MAKING IT
IN TOUGH TIMES

Pamela Wagaman

ISBN:1-4392-1810-2

ISBN-13: 9781439218105

Library of Congress Control Number: 2008910342

Visit www.booksurge.com to order additional copies.

Introduction

The idea for this book came about during the presidential campaign of 2008, just after the second presidential debate. Even before these debates, it had become clear that not only America, but the world, was facing escalating crises. The disparity between overabundance and starvation has become dramatic, with millions dying from lack of basic food while at the same time, obesity has become epidemic on several continents. As some children are desperate for a simple meal, others have become so overweight that they are developing diseases previously seen only in adults (such as type 2 diabetes, known a generation ago as adult onset diabetes). The increased incidence of infection with superbugs and viral strains, many previously limited to lands far from home, has become commonplace in our country.

The global warming crisis has reached epic proportions. One graphic example of global warming effects is the impact of receding Arctic sea ice on polar bears. These animals need polar ice during the spring for hunting seals and for birthing and caring for their cubs. However the polar ice cap has been thawing earlier in recent years, thinning and receding. As a result, the bears are starving, drowning, and producing fewer offspring. Indigenous people who have hunted polar bears for fur and food are also affected, as hunting quotas for the animals have declined by 85% since 2006 in some areas.

Now, at the end of 2008, we look forward to the inauguration of our new president. Meanwhile, the news is dominated by efforts to follow the trails of failed banks, government- (and thus taxpayer-) sponsored bailouts, rapidly rising unemployment, foreclosure and bankruptcy, and plans for government takeover of failed megacompanies. The stock market has tumbled over 30% during the past year. People everywhere are either already going under for the third time or wondering if they are next.

Analysts and politicians everywhere are busy pointing fingers, scrambling to assess and control the economic damage and put out fires. Meanwhile, you and I and the people on our street and in our families have work to do to get through this crisis at home. So I want to share some ideas for getting through the tough times ahead for all of us.

I initially imagined putting together my ideas to share with my family, and as a way to restructure my own plan for the next several years as I rethink retirement. But managing the financial crunch will take more than just making a list. All of us will need to pull together, help each other, share ideas, and get back to basics. There are people all around us who have been through very tough times—health crises, divorce or bankruptcy, war, and immigration—and have made it. These are the people who can help guide us through this crisis.

So what do I bring to the table? I am an elder, born just before the end of World War II. One of my first crises was the death of my father when I was seventeen. My thirty-nine-year-old, stay-at-home mother was left with four children aged six through seventeen. She already had some of the tools to weather tough times, having grown up during the Great Depression in rural Mississippi. She has told me of cousins coming to live with her family of five children, and of my grandmother making extra pies to leave on the porch for hungry travelers. As part of a middle-class American family, I was unaware of financial hardships before my father died. My mother began working outside the home, and my sisters and I shared cooking and cleaning duties as we adjusted to life with one parent. I took a part time job, the first of several that would help me achieve my goal of graduating from college.

Later, my husband and I weathered the usual ups and downs every young family faces, doing what was needed to raise our children. I was divorced at age forty-nine, with a young teen still at home and two daughters in college, and began a late career the following year.

My first year as a single mom was tough. I worked two jobs and moved into an apartment with my youngest daughter. That first Christmas, I was unsure that I would have the money or the energy to create any magic.

I still remember the tears of disbelief and gratitude I felt while driving home one night with my gift for my young daughter. I also purchased a small, potted lemon tree, complete with fruit, and decorated it with a string of miniature lights. When my older girls returned home from college for the holiday, the tiny decorated lemon tree dropped a leaf every time someone came through the front door. In retrospect, I have many warm feelings and funny stories from those tough times. There are a few sad stories, too; but mostly I feel very strong.

Now, after being forced into early retirement and still job shopping a year later, I am watching in horror as my retirement funds drop out of sight in a market out of control. I am hearing the forecast that people like me will need to postpone retirement. But many of us are already out of work, and over two million workers have been laid off in 2008 alone. I will need to tap into all the tools I have to get through this crisis!

I have no doubt that Americans will face several tough years. But we are creative and hardworking people. It took our country a long time to get into this financial mess, and it will take a long time for our elected officials to devise and implement a plan to get us out. In the meantime, I offer some ideas for restructuring your own life to get through this crisis. I have collected some of these ideas from family and friends, or have found them in written material or on the Web. Many are ideas that have helped me to get through tough times. My hope is that anyone—retirees and those living on a fixed income or disability, the newly divorced, those living with serious health or financial issues—will be able to use some of the ideas offered in this book.

We will need to work together with friends and loved ones to change the way we live and the way we spend the resources we do have. We need to learn to simplify, get back to basics, make a plan and roll up our sleeves. My plan is to offer some ideas, tell you about some things that have worked for me in the past, and share some references (books, websites, and recipes) to stimulate your imagination. If Americans are anything, we are strong and innovative. So take what you can use, get ready for some new adventures, and join me as we dive into the tough times!

Chapter One

Getting Started—Hey, Honey, Do We Really Need This?

Before you can design a plan that will work for you, it will be important to spend some time taking a serious look at your finances and evaluating your current life plan. You'll need checkbooks, bank statements, any budgeting materials you've worked on previously, several hours of undisturbed time, paper or a computer, and plenty of coffee. This is the time to get a firm grip on reality, look your spending habits in the face, and brainstorm about ways to save money and make a new life. Remember, there are no wrong answers when you brainstorm—just get it all out on the table.

Make a list of all income you can count on right now. If you are unemployed, are you collecting unemployment benefits? How long can you continue to collect? Be sure to include whatever savings you can tap into. If you do not have a budget, this is the time to look at fixed monthly or quarterly expenditures. Just get all the facts down, without discussion. How much do you spend on grocery store runs and utilities? Sports or lessons for the family? Quick trips for fast food? Gasoline and transportation costs, entertainment, medical expenses, pets, hobbies?

Now go through this list and draw a line through everything that you can do without. This is all very personal, and it also depends on how much you plan to downsize during the economic crisis. Personal story:

I recently opted to let go of my study of T'ai Chi, an important part of my life for ten years. It was a painful decision, but I will save money, practice alone or with a friend, and then review my budget in a year, knowing that I can go back when funds are available again.

Remember, this evaluation process will undoubtedly take several days, and you will need to massage your new budget to get a workable plan. Your new budget won't be fixed in stone—you may want to rework it as economic conditions become easier or if you need to tighten your belt even more. A lot of this budgeting process consists of looking at what is really important to you, or to each person in your family. Be sure to include small ways to celebrate accomplishments during this process, so you don't feel overwhelmed or cheated. If a total life change is too much, look at ways to cut back in smaller steps.

Next, examine each of the fixed expenses in your budget and begin to explore ways to reduce their cost. I will offer specific suggestions later in this book. Check out the resources at the end of the book, as well.

Talk with neighbors, family and friends about a way to share ideas; maybe by hosting a potluck or informal cookout. I've found that everyone I've talked with is terrified about the economic crisis and we are all struggling. Once a support network is established, you may decide to meet, say, once a quarter. As you try new ideas or find new resources, share them with your network.

Do We Really Need This?

I don't know about you, but my closets contain stuff I've accumulated with great intentions—scraps of fabric for quilts, pants I'd love to believe I might fit into some day, items in the kitchen I really meant to use in a new recipe but forgot about. I could probably eat for a couple of weeks out of my pantry and freezer, allowing for purchase of perishables.

$$ Make a plan to use up all items for which you have duplicates. Make soup from all of the dried beans. If you have pasta, try some new low-cost recipes! Anyone out there storing bars of great-smelling soap? Take inventory and use it until it's gone! This activity will get you through the first several weeks of cutting your expenses, and you'll feel great cleaning out the shelves and using the freed-up space for the necessities you will need to purchase in bulk for the coming months.

$$ Go through closets, garage, and storage areas in the kitchen. Find items you have not used in a year and consider a family or neighborhood garage sale. My experience is that these can sometimes make significant money, and sometimes not. The sales that worked best for me were those I organized with friends. During very busy times, several workers are a must to handle the confusion and questions from customers. A helper can be invaluable during quiet times, too, to help reorganize items and keep you company. Discuss the idea with your network partners to get their input.

If you decide to do a sale, be sure to find out if you need a day license, now required in many cities as more and more people unload their belongings! You'll need to post signs and advertise. Check in your city to see where you can advertise for no charge. Don't forget to stop at the bank for money to make change. For a group sale, prices can be written on painter's tape with initials of the seller. Then, at checkout, transfer the pieces of tape to a master sheet of paper, and settle up with your coworkers after the sale. And be prepared for early birds! I once had a driveway littered with cigarette butts and anxious shoppers waiting for me to open my garage an hour before the advertised start time.

\$\$ Another way to cut costs is to trade, or barter, goods that you no longer need. I have heard that this is a great way to get a new work wardrobe. Invite some friends to come to your place, maybe have a glass of wine or iced coffee, and check out each other's sweaters and slacks, negotiating trades for new items. Of course, this will be much more fun with a larger group, so tell each of your friends to bring a guest. Bartering is also a great way to exchange children's clothing and toys, electronic games, kitchen equipment or household items, lawn equipment, or extra produce from your garden.

Chapter Two

Kids' Issues—Dealing With Monsters
under the Bed

The Family Council

There is no quick fix for this financial crisis. Economic experts predict it will take months, or even several years, before the economy moves smoothly again. Making changes in the way we relate to money will affect the entire family, and if your family includes children, you will need the buy-in of the younger family members as well as the adults. One way of accomplishing this is to work as a team, and begin by setting up a family council.

What has worked for my family is to establish a few ground rules, then to meet periodically and agree that everyone will listen respectfully and at least consider the input and suggestions of the others.

That said, I will tell you that we made it clear from the outset that the family did not always function as a democracy! We found that the parental unit needed to discuss issues before meeting, to make sure the adults were on the same page. For our family, most negotiation centered around boundaries about when work would be done. Saturday mornings worked best for us, with adults and children getting chores finished so we could spend the rest of the weekend playing, relaxing, or doing projects. Older children may appreciate the freedom to do their chores earlier, if necessary, to avoid cramping their social plans.

If you have done your initial work in delineating where resources come from and how they are spent, you may be able to choose several areas in which the children can contribute and find ways for everyone to work together to meet some common objectives. Letting kids know that this will be an adventure, keeping things upbeat, and encouraging them to talk about their fears will be part of your job in setting up this team. For instance, some children may worry that they will not have the skills to do a job, or that they will be expected to spend the entire day working. Just showing them how to do a new task, or reminding them that time for chores will be over at lunch time, may help ease them into the routine.

I would suggest starting the process by brainstorming—gathering and sharing ideas. If you have never done this, you'll find it is a great way to get the ball rolling. Begin by selecting one or two areas in which a few changes are likely to make a significant savings for the budget. Choose someone to write down all the ideas that are thrown out, without any discussion. Remember, there are no right or wrong answers here—each way of looking at a problem may bring a new idea to someone else. Then, combine ideas that are similar, and have a discussion to decide which ones might involve too much time or extra expense to implement. See if you can choose two or three ideas to build on and come up with a plan for action. Most important, don't be afraid to change course and try something new! As time goes on, and everyone becomes more confident and gains new skills, this whole process will get easier.

Here are some suggestions for discussion. Look at the jobs it takes to make your home run the way everyone wants, and compare these with the available skills. You will probably find that some family members need a little on-the-job-training! A work chart, perhaps rotating jobs every month, posted where everyone can see it, will help cut down on nagging—everyone should know to check the chart! Yard work or plant care, laundry, helping with meals, basic room cleaning, and caring for pets are good places to start.

Don't be afraid to reduce allowances or put them on hold when the family income is reduced or on hold. Most important, keep everyone appropriately up to date with what's going on and acknowledge the help of the "team" in meeting goals and helping out during this difficult time. This will go a long way toward reducing fear, and the whole process will give younger family members confidence and tools to use when they have to face tough times as adults.

$$ Expenses of Parenting

Here are a few ideas for tackling the everyday expenses of raising kids today. First, look at lessons for children—music, martial arts and other sports, dance, etc.—and consider whether this is an area that could be massaged or eliminated for a short time to help balance the budget. Many after school community programs and faith communities offer such programs at lower cost than private lessons. Singing with a church choir, for example, is a great way to learn music while also learning teamwork. Used music instruments as well as sports equipment may be purchased at a great savings. Another idea is to hold a uniform exchange in your neighborhood or for your child's team. Or consider bartering. Bartering, or trading, offers a win-win deal for cleaning out stuff you no longer need and getting things you do need at no cash outlay.

Try to start a babysitting co-op, trading time with other parents. Setting up a play group for preschoolers is a similar idea—depending on the number of participants, you may be a host-parent (or have parent co-hosts) once every other month and get a couple of hours away in exchange. Set up a planning session with like-minded parents to establish a schedule, plans for snacks, and emergency contact information.

$$ Activities for children

Many books and websites are available with great ideas for entertaining children without spending a lot of money. Several ideas that worked for my children (and now are working for my grandchildren!) are: Use large boxes to decorate as trains or trucks, houses or forts, spaceships, etc.; set up a craft closet or shelf with old magazines, scissors, glue, paints and crayons, construction paper, clay, and other materials (the sky's the limit here!); and encourage children to write and produce plays and puppet shows (socks or small paper bags make wonderful puppets) or write and perform songs. In the kitchen, children can also make a huge variety of snacks, or, with an adult's help, they can make cookies, bread or soups. This is especially exciting if the kids are using produce they have helped grow in a "victory garden".

$$ Other expenses

To help offset routine health expenses, look for community clinics. Although there is usually a wait for services, such clinics often provide low-cost or free immunizations or well-child checkups. If you live in a city with a dental school, call about low-cost clinics for dental care. Consider arranging a neighborhood exchange for books, video games, and toys. You may also find that buying used children's clothing and toys is a quick way to trim the budget. Garage sales and co-ops are great places to shop for clothing, especially seasonal, high-cost items such as coats and snowsuits.

Chapter Three

Controlling Household Expenses

The cost of a place to live is one of the largest items on most people's budgets. We've all seen how the damage to the housing market and lending sector has taken such a huge toll on our lives. Our families and friends, and perhaps we ourselves, may be struggling to make rent or mortgage payments and facing possible bankruptcy. When combined with job loss, increased costs of home heating, and the costs of looking for new employment and feeding our loved ones, the financial pressure can be overwhelming. For those who have the available resources and can qualify for a home loan, of course, this is a great time to snap up bargains. For people who must ride out the next several years and may be using their savings just to make ends meet, I offer a few ideas for tightening your belt and downsizing.

$$ If you are renting a home, this is a perfect time to assess your needs and perhaps look for less expensive digs. Moving to a smaller home, a less costly neighborhood, a place closer to work, or a home without the expensive extra features may be a way to save a chunk of money each month. Be sure to look at all aspects of such a move, however. Moving costs, the emotional toll, and coming up with deposits may make this a less realistic option.

Rental subsidy programs are offered in some communities. These collaborations between federal, state, and local government, sometimes called Section 8

Rental Assistance Programs, provide housing for no more than 30 percent of the renter's income. Funding for these programs is competitive, so check with the local housing department in your community for availability.

$$ Consider the possibility of renting a room in a private home, or renting out a room in your own home to earn extra money. For a single or an older homeowner, this would be a great way to barter living space and kitchen privileges in exchange for help with your yard and transportation to appointments or the grocery. Be sure to carefully check references, and to write a simple contract so that both parties are on the same page! The contract will need to address specific expectations regarding such issues as guests, noise levels, smoking or alcohol use, and food expenditures.

$$ If you have the time and skills to manage an apartment complex, look into managing in exchange for living in your own unit rent-free. A dear friend has told me this works very well for men or women on a limited budget, especially retired people. My friend's experience was overall a positive one, although she admits that managing while also working another job was difficult. The owner of the property may expect you to coordinate repairs and deposit rental checks. A concern might be the possibility of late night interruptions from tenants, certainly an issue to discuss with the hiring manager.

$$ Are you paying someone to clean your house? This might be a luxury to scratch from the budget to save money. My suggestion is to set aside a specific time, say on Thursday evening or Saturday morning, to spend a couple of hours blasting through a cleaning routine. Here's what works for me: Have all your cleaning equipment organized and handy, put on some "moving" music (mine is Tina Turner, or music from the old movie "Flashdance"), and clean like a maniac for two hours. Stop working for a fifteen- to twenty-minute break, then finish by dusting, vacuuming, and cleaning floors. Laundry can be done while you are cleaning, if you do laundry at home. If you need to use a Laundromat, use that time to catch up on correspondence and bill paying. Set aside one day every three months or so to do large or seasonal jobs. If you pay someone to take care of your yard, this is the time to begin doing it yourself, assuming you have the basic tools and physical ability. Garage sales are great places to find deals on yard equipment!

$$ Be sure to turn off lights when not in use, adjust thermostats to conserve energy, wash clothing in cold water, and dry clothing outdoors or on indoor racks. Look at energy websites for sources of funding supplements, tax credits, and rebates for installing insulation or solar panels, or for purchasing energy-efficient appliances. Change the air filters on heating/air conditioning units to increase efficiency and save money. Also, clean the air intake on your refrigerator—this can usually be done with a bottle brush followed by vacuuming. (In the next chapter I will talk about the financial and ecological advantages of these practices.)

$$ A couple of additional ways to cut household costs are to prepare your own taxes and to assume more liability with insurance. Some of your expenses for a job

search may be tax deductible, so keep receipts for these expenses in an envelope or file to use for tax preparation. Review deductibles for car and homeowners insurance, and consider increasing the deductible rate. You may find that increasing these, and thus assuming more of the risk yourself, will save you big bucks. Also review your policies to be sure you have the proper mileage for travel to work, and to see if there are possible discounts you may be missing, such as those for insuring both home and car with one insurance provider. If you own your home and the property value has decreased significantly during the housing crisis, contact city hall in your area to ask about abatements for property taxes. Special property tax exemptions may also be available for the elderly or for those who meet income requirements.

Chapter Four

Energy Usage

Energy use and its impact on global climate effects and economics, have become hot (pardon the pun!) topics. Here are some of the very basic issues. We are in hock to the Chinese government for billions of dollars that we send to the Persian Gulf and OPEC members, so that we can continue to purchase oil that helps us ruin the environment. Got it?

Approximately 30 percent of our oil usage is for automobiles. Most people in the American middle class drive large vehicles, such as SUVs, vans, or trucks that consume large amounts of gasoline. In addition, we generally drive (alone) to work, and think nothing of taking the car for spur-of-the-moment errands to pick up fast food or make a run to the hardware store or bookstore.

Our food may be shipped cross-country so that we can, in the name of instant gratification, enjoy produce out of season. As a matter of fact, a significant portion of the cost of many foods is for transportation! Many of the foods we eat in the United States are shipped, on average, fifteen hundred to twenty-five hundred miles to reach market. Energy usage for transportation, as well as for temperature control, and storage contribute to the high costs of food items—even more reasons to purchase locally produced food.

Working together to heal the planet should be a top priority for us, but it will require the same kind of passion and dedication that will be needed to get us through the tough financial crisis we are facing. The truth is, beginning to form new habits for energy usage now will help us begin to heal the planet as well as save money to get us through these tough times. Al Gore has started us thinking about living "green"—if you have not been paying attention, this is the time to begin! He has given us plenty of ideas, and a few are mentioned below to get you started.

$$ Begin with the power usage in your home. Use only power-saver bulbs to replace light bulbs as they burn out, and be sure to turn off lights, televisions, etc. when not in use. Minimize usage of heating and air conditioning. In cold weather, wear warmer clothing and set the thermostat lower; turn the heat down even lower when you are sleeping. Plan meals so that oven usage or cooking of stews or soups will help provide warmth to the home. Take a serious inventory of the energy efficiency of your home—have an inspection done, if possible, to see where insulation (ceiling, walls, floors), caulking around doors and windows, or usage of small space heaters might save money. In rooms that receive plenty of sunlight, open curtains and blinds during hours with maximum sunlight during cold weather, then close them late in the afternoon to help hold in the warmth. Consider leaving pans of water in some rooms, or even running a humidifier, to increase humidity and thus increase the feeling of warmth.

In moderate weather, open windows if possible, and turn off climate control. In hot weather, avoid cooking during the hottest part of the day—this is a great time to enjoy salads and other cool meals several days each week. Try meals that require only quick cooking, like stir-fry with all that fresh summer produce, or grill meats and veggies outdoors. Ceiling fans, if you have them, can be used to keep air moving, and thermostats can generally be adjusted so that if air conditioning is used, it can be set at a higher temperature. Keep window coverings closed during the hottest part of the day.

Sorry—I've lived most of my life in the southeast and Southern California, so I know little to nothing about warming homes with wood stoves! I do know that they are extremely popular for heating the living areas of homes, and in some areas of the northeastern United States they are difficult to find due to increased demand. Look in the newspaper, or share-sites online, for free or low cost wood.

$$ Transportation

Besides making serious strides toward curbing energy usage to save our beautiful planet, a few equally serious attitude changes can keep some extra cash in our pockets and help with balancing the budget. Some suggestions: If you must purchase a vehicle, buy a used one if possible. The value of a new vehicle drops considerably just by driving it away from the dealer. Pay attention to the gas mileage. Several newer hybrid cars are now on the market which, unlike the earlier prototypes, have enough pickup to get you off the interstate on-ramp as well as lower emissions and more efficient gasoline usage. So you can save money on gas bills while helping to protect the environment.

Consider public transportation if you live in a medium or large city. Use of monthly passes can save money and passes are often discounted for students and elders. In my city, a monthly bus pass costs less than half a tank of bargain-priced regular gas. Other ways to save big bucks are to walk whenever possible, or to use a bicycle or motorbike. My son-in-law is a very serious bicycle fan, and uses bicycle commuting most days as a way to clock road time. Riding a bicycle is also a great way to reduce stress and, in urban areas, to avoid traffic jams.

Carpooling is another way to save money and cut down on fuel usage and emissions. Some employers reserve special parking spaces for those who carpool, and carpool lanes may be available in your area to improve traffic flow. Check with your employer or delegated websites in your area to find people interested in carpooling. You will also need to have a backup plan in case someone needs to work late or leave early for an emergency.

Another way to cut gas usage (already used by many folks) is to prioritize errands—consider whether a quick trip can be postponed and combined with other errands. Plan your route in advance, prioritizing stops, even making a list to keep you on course. Your last stop should be for picking up items that need to be kept cold, so you can get them home before they thaw. Gasoline is a huge budget item for many people, so making the lifestyle changes needed to really cut down on gas usage will pay off, although it may require some serious attitude adjustments and coordination!

Chapter Five

Food

A high ticket item

The costs of housing and energy have risen to frightening levels, and are fixed items that form the core of most budgets. Food costs, too, have continued to rise while more than two million people have lost their jobs during 2008. Whether you live alone or have others to feed, there are a variety of ways to begin changing food habits with the goal of eating delicious, healthful meals and still saving money. Only you can decide how serious the budget cuts must be and which items are non-negotiables. It may take several weeks to establish new habits and try a few new recipes, but these changes can make a very real difference in money spent.

Begin by honestly examining some of your food habits. Do you hate to cook, or eat out to avoid eating alone or to save time? How much of your food expenditure is for specialty items, or for perishables that turn into science experiments before reaching the table? To get a visual of your eating habits, try keeping a detailed food diary for a couple of weeks while you gather food plans and recipes. When I tried this, I found I could save over fifty dollars each month just by taking my own food to work.

Prepare and consume meals at home to carve some real expense from your food budget. You will eat more healthfully and get more nutrition for your hard-earned money.

$$ Ready to begin saving?

One way to save money on food is to use coupons. Another is to look in the newspaper, on the Web, and in circulars for specials. This is a reasonable way to begin saving money on stock items. Just be sure that you are not canceling savings by driving to several locations, using time and energy, just to save a negligible amount of cash.

Switching to generic or house brands of some items can save considerable money, and often there is little difference from other brands besides the label and advertising. Purchase bulk items only if you have room to store them, you will actually use the items, and they won't spoil. For example, stock up on large packages of bathroom tissue, laundry detergent, and bath soap when you find them at special prices. Compare the cost per load of laundry for dry and liquid detergent. Liquid detergent is often more expensive (as well as heavier to carry).

Staples such as rice or oatmeal may be purchased at some markets or co-ops in amounts needed for a month or so and stored in plastic storage bins.

$$ Explore new ways of eating

Instead of paying four dollars a box for processed dry cereal, try cooking hot cereal. Cook the cereal with a little chopped dried fruit or raisins to sweeten it. And there are so many different grains out there to test! Look for some that are new to you, such as millet, grits, or quinoa.

For the noon meal, make it a point to eat leftovers and to pack bag lunches. Think picnic food—finger food such as fresh fruits and veggies, spiced bean spreads or nut or seed butters with whole grain breads or crackers make fun, nutritious, and inexpensive additions to lunch bags.

For a really fun adventure that includes high-protein, healthful, and value-packed meals, explore ethnic recipe ideas. People in many parts of the world have found combinations of foods that provide balanced meals for very little money. For example, experiment with coarsely ground corn meal, or polenta. This can be prepared for pennies, poured into a baking dish to chill and set, then stored in the fridge and cut into squares before browning in olive oil and serving with any number of yummy toppings. Polenta is a staple in many upscale restaurants! Foods from South America and the Middle East are also good sources of inexpensive nutrition. And don't forget about high protein tofu and tempeh while you are on this incredible food journey!

Compare the costs of various cuts of meats and purchase less expensive cuts. Truthfully, humans do not need to consume as much meat as we Americans eat.

Meat is a high-cost item when you factor in production and transportation. Eating meat is also a deceptively easy way to consume too many calories and fat, leading to expensive health issues. I have included some wonderful, fun-to-read books on the topic in the Resources section as well as several cookbooks to give you new meal planning ideas.

Finally, stop paying for sodas and flavored beverages loaded with high-fructose corn syrup. Although the soft drink industry has made many of its products more affordable by sweetening with high-fructose corn syrup, water or tea is a less expensive and much healthier alternative. Large containers of these beverages may be flavored with a little sugar, honey, fruit juice or sucralose and kept available in the fridge.

Now let's be brutally honest–how much do you really spend each month on specialty coffee drinks? Man,

I love those things, but they add up to a lot of bucks! Try flavoring your coffee at home. Make an iced coffee with milk and a splash of vanilla. Or perk your favorite coffee (or a cheaper brand) with one-half teaspoon ground cinnamon mixed into the ground coffee. If you still miss the luxury of the coffee house, allow yourself a store-bought coffee treat, say, once a month, or every Friday on the way to work (TGIF!).

$$ Do-it-yourself

Look at your eating habits or that of your family to see whether it makes sense to prepare some items at home. For example, in my household of two adults, we eat a lot of yogurt, so making it ourselves saves about ten dollars per month. It's great with fresh, seasonal fruit and a sprinkle of homemade granola, and can be used as a healthful substitute for sour cream on baked potatoes.

Depending on the size of your household, some items, like bread, may be more economical to purchase ready-made. Look for bakery outlets or for day-old whole-grain breads in your supermarket.

Start a "victory garden." Grow some or most of your own produce—bumper crops can be given to food banks, shared or traded with others, or processed and stored for out-of-season staples. If you have a yard, this is a great way to save money and eat healthfully—one of the big lessons from those who lived during the Great Depression. I have had a wonderful experience with my community garden plot. Compost, mulch, and water are available onsite, covered by a setup fee. Gardening is also a great intergenerational activity, and it provides a ready supply of seasonal produce and herbs for the kitchen. There are more and more community garden plots being started across America. Check the Internet or talk with neighbors and friends for ideas or locations since many gardens have long waiting lists. Even on a small balcony you can grow chard and kale, tomatoes, and herbs in pots.

Eat produce that is in season and, if possible, locally grown. Asparagus and strawberries are spring produce; when you buy them in winter, you will pay a premium for the petroleum products it took to get them to you! Eggplants, zucchini, cucumbers and tomatoes are summer crops—so load up on ratatouille (to eat either hot or cold) and then wait until next summer for the next splurge. Again, check out some of the cookbooks and other reference materials in the Resources section for loads of other ideas to inspire you. Bon appetit!

Chapter Six

Entertainment—Playing on a Budget

I see entertainment as a getaway, a little down time to refresh the spirit, a way to avoid feeling deprived during tough times, and also as a learning experience. It is a way to revive the spirit and celebrate our humanity. Loads of opportunities exist for low-cost or free ways to "get away" for an hour or an afternoon—check the newspaper and local neighborhood rags, and, of course, chat with the people in your support network! The ideas below are just the beginning.

$$ Arrange family or neighborhood afternoons of play and include a potluck. If you have enough people, try for team games like volleyball or softball. Or sit and share ideas with the adults while younger neighbors play. Family or neighbor game nights, with everyone bringing a favorite game and treat, or popcorn and movie night, could also be fun without spending a lot of money.

$$ If you have been spending extra cash online or in local bookstores, this is a perfect time to get a library card! Public libraries are very busy places, with media and activities for all ages, and with reference materials as well as computer access in many facilities. In addition to books, you can borrow video games, movies, and music, and join discussion groups and reading clubs for children or adults. There are all sorts of exciting activities. And most libraries are temperature controlled—comfortable places to read or surf the Web in extreme weather.

$$ Speaking of movies, you might want to purchase used copies of your favorite movies. For family movie night, why not plan an intergenerational show, with G-rated movies early and more adult, political or action themes after little ones have been put to sleep. Don't forget the popcorn!

$$ Low-cost tickets to concerts, plays and other performances can usually be found with a little investigation. For theater and concerts, stay alert for promotional performances and special discounts, especially for military personnel, retirees, and students. Most medium-to-large cities have designated locations or programs for the purchase of bargain tickets. Call individual venues about special ticket prices offered just before showtime (this can be an adventure!). Or plan to attend matinee performances or specially discounted dress rehearsals. Remember to check neighborhood newspapers for special or free performances at churches, universities, community centers, bookstores and coffee houses.

$$ If the visual arts are your passion, keep informed about openings at small local art galleries—often free, usually with light refreshments, and an opportunity to meet the artists and local supporters of the arts. The art departments of universities and community colleges often sponsor openings as well. Check with art museums, or other museums, in your town for free days or activities.

$$ Volunteer! In my city, being a volunteer at the natural history museum opens the door for great free or minimal-cost activities such as lectures, exhibits, movies, and other fun happenings, in addition to opportunities to learn new skills and meet new people. Those who volunteer to serve as ushers for concerts and theatrical productions may also see the performances free, just for guiding people to their seats, passing out programs, and handling the doors—a great tradeoff in my book!

$$ For outdoor activities, look for opportunities for hiking, gardening, star-gazing, or tide pooling (if you live on the coast), meteor showers (in August and early winter), events in parks and national preserves, and similar money-saving activities. You can find information about these opportunities on dedicated websites. Larger plant nurseries usually offer free lectures on gardening or working outdoors. And if you live near a natural history museum or urban science center, check their programs for free lectures, films, hikes, and other programs.

$$ Free or low-cost programs may be found in some cities for learning T'ai Chi or yoga, country/Western dancing, writing, or art. Check your local newspaper for these—they are activities that require little expenditure and may be practiced at home, in your yard, or outdoors in a park. An extra benefit is that these activities may help reduce stress, especially during these tough times. Just a few hours in a quiet park can be used to read, walk, meditate, sleep or play Frisbee. And don't forget that during the holidays the numbers of opportunities for free or low-cost activities will multiply!

Chapter Seven

Keeping in Touch—Giving and Receiving Support

$$ Communication

Until we need to go on an extreme austerity program (which I've had to do a couple of times), having easy access to both business contacts and loved ones is a good idea. You can still save some money by prioritizing use of communication tools. Here are a couple of quick ways to tighten the budget.

First, if you have both a home telephone and a cell phone, decide which gives you more flexibility and is most economical, then cancel the other. Be sure to notify your family and support network! Also, consider canceling cable television if you have this, or change your plan to a less expensive one that offers fewer options.

I don't know about you, but I am still looking for a job, so I will keep my Internet access. This lets me search and apply for jobs online and receive notices of potential employment. It is also my personal way to stay connected, do research, and write. But for some, getting rid of this luxury is a great way to save money.

Join an electronic card club. Joining costs about as much for one year as buying and mailing two greeting cards (less if you consider the cost of transportation to get the cards and drive to the post office!). With the clubs, you can set up reminder lists and import your electronic address book. I've found that most people understand tough times and when they receive a card and personal message rather than a gift, most are just happy to be remembered.

$$ Gift-giving

Remembering special times (anniversaries, birthdays, holidays) with a gift may be particularly challenging when you are trying to manage a budget on unemployment checks, Social Security, or reduced paychecks. Here are a few ideas to stimulate your imagination.

Homemade gifts can be economical and personal, and may be treats from the kitchen or craft items. Small but useful gifts are also very thoughtful. These can include small bottles of a special olive oil or flavored vinegar, teas or coffees, wine, jams or honeys. Other suggestions are lotions and soaps, kitchen linens, bookmarks, or small picture frames with a favorite snapshot or school picture.

For a special celebration, invite someone to your home for a memorable meal—this might be a dinner, small luncheon, or brunch. Cut flowers make a very special gift that many people would not purchase for themselves during hard times, and potted plants can also be purchased or potted from your own plant collection. For holiday celebrations, holiday ornaments, whether purchased or homemade, make very nice gifts, as do candles.

What has worked for many families or groups of friends is to call a truce on gift giving, perhaps going together to work at a soup kitchen, visiting or reading to some older people who may not have holiday visitors, or making a living donation to someone in another country (see Resources). As an example of such a special donation, my sister purchased a piglet one Christmas, through a charitable foundation, to be given to a family in a South

American village. Then she sent a note with an ornament shaped like a pig to each family member. Some families or groups agree to present holiday gifts only to children, to draw names, or to have a "white elephant" gift exchange. The most important gift, you will find, is the time spent together!

One more idea—print and decorate gift cards as certificates of your time. You might offer two hours of babysitting, a weekend of pet sitting, to cook the recipient's favorite meal, to give a hot rock massage, or to do some landscaping. Just be creative—it will be easy once the ideas start flowing!

Chapter Eight

Lagniappe

On the Gulf Coast, where Hurricane Katrina put so many people through some very tough times, you might hear someone speak of lagniappe. This is a little something extra—such as an extra, free donut when you purchase a dozen. So here are a few extra ideas, ones that did not fit into a specific category, to spark your creativity while looking for ways to trim that budget and keep spirits up during the economic challenges ahead.

$$ Switch away from use of credit to a cash economy. Use a debit card, prepaid card, or, as Lucy of *Peanuts* fame prefers, cold hard cash—do everything in your power to avoid using credit! One way of losing control of your monthly (or weekly) budget is to make snap decisions about the "need" for certain goods or services and put them on credit. We all do it—maybe rationalizing that we have worked hard and deserve a little something, or not thinking about how the purchase fits into our new money-saving plans.

$$ When you are tempted to splurge, just walk away—go for a walk, get a cup of coffee, or call a buddy from your support network who can listen as you discuss your possible purchase. Is this an item you really need right now, or can the purchase be postponed until the financial crisis is less extreme? Have you done some homework, comparing prices and quality of similar items? What is the plan for paying for the item? Once you can answer these questions, at least you are making a more informed decision about the purchase.

$$ For some folks, hair and nail care may be an expense that can be temporarily trimmed (so to speak!). If you are in a high-profile job or searching for employment, an inexpensive but professional cut may be very important not only for appearances but for your self-esteem. But special services such as weekly nail jobs, hair color, and waxing can be quite expensive and a drain on a tight budget. Give some thought to whether they are necessary and, if so, how you may be able to cut costs, such as using student services, trading skills with a friend, or doing it yourself.

$$ If you are in college or a training program, consider ways to cut some of your largest expenses. Can you take a year away from your studies to work full-time and bank the cash or to volunteer to help others who may be struggling with the economic crisis? Have you looked into internships in your area of study? Some of these pay a stipend, and you may be able to receive academic credit for the on-the-job training. If you are just getting started, how about picking up your core courses at a local or community college, then transferring to a larger school after a couple of years? This might also allow you to work part time and, if you are living at home, stash the cash for expenses once you transfer. Of course, some expenses can be trimmed by purchasing used books, downloading books from the publisher, or sharing books with a study buddy.

Finally, talk with someone who might have special insight into living in tough times. Grandparents or great-grandparents, other friends, or relatives who lived through the Great Depression may have all kinds of hints for saving money and getting through a crisis or long, difficult times. Others who may have special insight into solving problems are those who were alive during World War II or immigrants who have come to America to start over. Some of them have escaped war, hunger, loss of family members, and even torture. Many are struggling here, as well, to begin a new life. Those who have been through a divorce or a health crisis may also be able to give you pointers on setting priorities and making ends meet.

Chapter Nine

Wrapping It Up—You Can Do This!

There is absolutely no doubt that we are experiencing some of the most difficult times in decades. The scary, disorienting economic events seem to change daily and are the topics of conversation at water coolers, at church and social events, and around kitchen tables across America. So many people have not only themselves to care for, but elders and children as well. Many people have lost their jobs or had their work hours reduced. Some were already retired or on disability, struggling to maintain control of their budgets with the cost of living spiraling out of control. And some, like me, were only a year or two away from a simple retirement for which they had worked, planned, and saved for years, only to watch helplessly as it all slipped away. Over the last six months, I kept thinking, *Hey, what about those people we elected to take care of business in Washington? Who's been watching the store?!*

While many huge decisions will be made by those at the political and economic helm, and while we must at some level begin to trust their abilities to do their homework and make the big decisions that ultimately affect our lives, we must shoulder some of the responsibility and get on with the business of handling the work we can do at home. My personal feeling is that we have all been through tough times, and we already have many of the tools to tighten our belts and make it through this crisis.

Getting through these times will be very hard work, and often frightening and discouraging. There won't be any quick fixes. It took us years to get into this financial mess, and will take a long time to turn around. Financial analysts have assured us it will take years, not a month or two, to repair the damage. But Americans are creative, crazy, hardworking, innovative people. We will make it and will be stronger for dealing with the times.

I expect life will look very different on the other side of the current economic crisis. But I choose to believe that we will be much better off when we finally come through the tough times. Life will be simpler as we get back to basics. We may be healthier, if we've started eating more nutritious food (and less of it), and getting outdoors to walk and play. We have the opportunity to enjoy more quality time with family and friends, and strengthen those bonds as we pitch in to share ideas and talents. And we might rebuild communication skills (or develop new ones) as we simplify our lives and engage in conversations and sharing our thoughts and feelings. Most of all, we can revitalize that tough, roll-up-your-sleeves attitude that makes Americans so strong, and leave the next generation with the tools and strength to get through today as well as prepare for future tough times.

Resources

<u>Books</u>

Pollan, Michael. *The Omnivore's Dilemma: A Natural History of Four Meals*. Penguin Books, 2006.

Kingsolver, Barbara, Steven L. Hopp, and Camille Kingsolver. *Animal, Vegetable, Miracle: A Year of Food Life*. Harper Collins Publishers, 2007.

Gore, Al. *An Inconvenient Truth: The Planetary Emergency of Global Warming and What We Can Do About It*. Rodale, 2006.

Robertson, Robin. *Vegan Planet: 400 Irresistible Recipes with Fantastic Flavors from Home and Around the World.* The Harvard Common Press, 2003.

Medearis, Angela Shelf. *The Ethnic Vegetarian: Traditional and Modern Recipes from Africa, America, and the Caribbean.* Rodale, 2004.

Salloum, Habeeb. *Classic Vegetarian Cooking From the Middle East and North Africa.* Interlink Books, 2000.

Websites

www.craigslist.org Worldwide links to want ads, services, discussion groups, and housing

www.freecycle.org A nonprofit, worldwide network to reuse unwanted items and keep them out of landfills www.PlanMyGreen.com Information on energy

conservation and alternative energy sources

www1.eere.energy.gov/informationcenter U.S.

Department of Energy website on energy efficiency and

renewable energy

www.creativekidsathome.com Free ideas for children's

crafts, activities, games, and science projects

www.laptoplunches.com Website includes suggestions

and menus for healthy lunches

www.heifer.org An international humanitarian

organization that fights hunger around the world with

donations of gift animals and seedlings

www.mindspring.com/~communitygardens/ A resource guide for funding, starting and managing an urban community garden

Favorite Recipes

Ratatouille

¼ cup olive oil

2-3 cloves garlic, minced

1 medium onion, chopped

1 green bell pepper, chopped

1 medium eggplant, unpeeled and cubed

1 ½ cups chopped fresh tomato OR 1 15-oz can diced
tomatoes

¼ cup finely chopped mixed fresh basil and oregano (or 1
Tbsp total if using dried herbs)

Heat olive oil in 2-quart cooking pot, add onion and garlic
and cook on medium heat, stirring, until onions begin to
clear. Add eggplant and pepper and continue to stir until

eggplant begins to cook—about 5 minutes. Add tomatoes (and a little water, if using fresh tomatoes), reduce heat, and cook covered over low heat for about 20 minutes. Add herbs, salt to taste, and continue cooking for 10 minutes. Serve hot or cold.

Polenta and Black Beans

Cooked, chilled polenta or grits

Canned black beans (or Cuban black beans)

Cheese

Cilantro, salsa

Cook polenta or grits according to package directions and pour into a square glass baking dish to about 1 inch deep. Chill and store in refrigerator. When ready to assemble, cut polenta into squares and brown in olive oil. Top with a slice of cheese, ½ cup of black beans, and serve with salsa and cilantro.

Zucchini Pasta

½ lb bowtie or penne pasta, cooked

2 Tbsp olive oil

½ medium onion, chopped

2-3 cloves garlic, minced

2 cups shredded fresh zucchini

1 cup chopped fresh tomato

1 Tbsp capers (or chopped olives)

Shredded Parmesan cheese

Chopped English walnuts or toasted pine nuts for garnish

Heat olive oil in large frying pan; cook garlic and onions until they begin to clear. Add zucchini and cook, while stirring, for about 3 minutes. Add tomatoes, cover, and cook on reduced heat until tomatoes are hot—about 5 minutes. Add 2-3 Tbsp water or broth if needed to keep juicy. Stir in capers. To serve, spoon vegetables over a bed of pasta, sprinkle with Parmesan cheese, and top with garnish.

Dr. Mom's Muesli

½ cup regular uncooked oats, soaked 30 minutes in ½ cup orange juice or milk

2 large shredded wheat biscuits, crumbled

½ cup toasted wheat germ

½ cup sliced almonds

1 large apple, shredded

1 large orange, cubed

1 banana, sliced

½ cup dried fruit (apricots, cranberries, or raisins are good)

¼ cup honey

Plain yogurt

Combine nuts, grains, and fruit; toss with honey until everything is coated. Serve about ½ cup of muesli topped with a large scoop of yogurt.

Breakfast Sundae

Serve ½ cup chopped seasonal fruit with ½ cup yogurt, sprinkled with granola.

About the Author

Pamela Wagaman began her career in the clinical laboratory before staying at home with her children for ten years. She returned to university to earn a Ph.D. in microbiology and spent sixteen years doing research and teaching. Dr. Wagaman currently lives in San Diego.

Notes